THE NATURE KIDS GUIDE TO
HONEY BADGERS

DAVID ANDERSON

LP Media Inc. Publishing
Text copyright © 2026 by LP Media Inc.

For information address LP Media Inc. Publishing,
30012 Variolite St NW, Princeton MN 55371
www.lpmedia.org

Publication Data

Honey Badgers
The Nature Kid's Guide to Honey Badgers — First edition.

Summary: "Learn all about Honey Badgers, the Nature Kid Way"
— Provided by publisher.

ISBN: 979-8-89818-131-4

[1. Honey Badgers – Non-Fiction] I. Title.

Title: The Nature Kid's Guide to Honey Badgers

CONTENTS

HARSH HOMES

DID YOU KNOW?

Honey badgers can dig a hiding burrow in just 10 minutes! They use their strong claws to dig fast!

Growl! A honey badger crawls out of a dark hole. It is ready to explore.

Honey badgers make their homes in hot deserts and dry grasslands. Some live in thick forests. Others live on rocky hills.

These animals dig **burrows**. Burrows keep them cool. The holes protect them from heat. They also block the cold. Some honey badgers use old holes. Other animals made these holes first.

Honey badgers can live where water is hard to find. They get water from their food so they rarely need to drink. This helps them live in dry lands.

BADGER BOUNDS

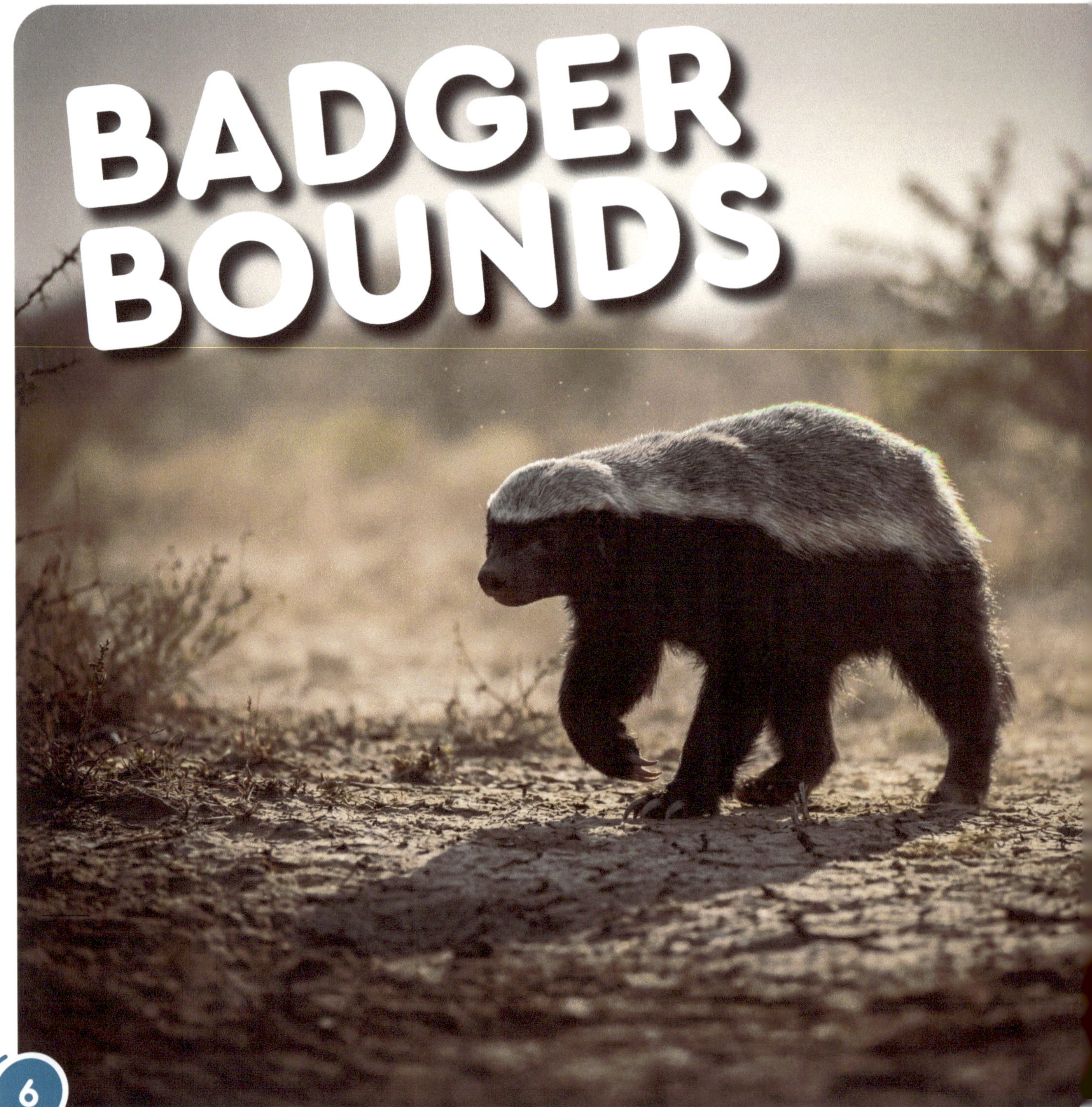

Snap! A honey badger trots across dry African soil.

Honey badgers live in Africa and Asia. In Africa, they live in over 30 countries! They roam from the southern tip all the way up to Morocco. They skip the middle of the Sahara Desert, where it is too dry even for them!

In Asia, honey badgers live in the Middle East and India. Some even live near the mountains of Nepal.

Few animals live in as many countries as the honey badger.

Honey badgers have a habitat range that stretches over 7,000 miles.

SMALL BUT FIERCE

Thump! A honey badger waddles past a tall antelope.

Honey badgers are about the same height as a house cat. They stand only 10 inches tall at the shoulder.

They weigh between 20 and 35 pounds, but males are bigger than females. A large male can be twice as heavy as a small female.

Honey badgers have short legs and wide bodies. This strong build helps them fight and dig.

A honey badger is 2 to 2.5 feet long. Its tail adds 6 to 12 more inches.

BUILT TOUGH

DID YOU KNOW?
A honey badger's claws never stop growing. Digging wears them down to stay sharp.

Crunch! A honey badger bites through a tortoise shell.

Honey badgers have powerful jaws. Their teeth can crack hard shells and bones. They also have sharp claws that grow up to 1.5 inches long.

Their skulls are thick and strong. This protects their brain during fights. Their flat heads also help them move through tunnels.

Honey badgers have loose, rubbery skin. If a predator grabs them, they can twist around and bite back. This makes them hard to hold.

Their strong front legs help them dig fast. They can disappear underground in minutes.

SNIFF IT
OUT

Sniff! A honey badger lifts its nose to the air. What does it smell?

Honey badgers have an amazing sense of smell. They can sniff out prey hiding underground. Their noses find food even in total darkness.

Their small ears are hidden under thick skin. This protects them in fights! They can hear insects moving under the soil. They can even hear bees buzzing inside a hive from far away.

Honey badgers have poor eyesight. They rely on smell and sound instead.

Honey badgers have a special see-through eyelid that protects their eyes like a shield!

14

Snarl! A lion tries to bite a honey badger. The badger twists free and runs off!

Honey badgers have very thick skin. Around their neck and back, it can be about a quarter inch thick!

This tough skin stops bites and stings. Bee stingers rarely poke through. Even porcupine quills have trouble getting in.

The skin is also loose and stretchy. This lets them turn inside their own skin to escape danger.

Honey badger skin is so tough that arrows and spears often bounce off!

HUNGRY HUNTERS
16

Chomp! A honey badger eats a scorpion. The sting does not hurt it!

Honey badgers eat almost anything. They hunt over 60 kinds of animals. They catch snakes, frogs, and lizards.

They love **venomous** snakes. Cobras are a favorite. Puff adders are too. Their bodies protect them from snake venom.

They also eat fruits and berries. They eat honey from bee hives. They even snack on bird eggs!

Honey badgers hunt small mammals as well. They catch mice and rabbits.

Honey badgers can eat a whole snake in 15 minutes!

DIG DEEP

FUN FACT!
Honey badgers sometimes dig into termite mounds to eat thousands of termites in one meal!

18

Scratch! A honey badger digs fast. Dirt flies everywhere!

Honey badgers are expert diggers. Their strong front legs and long, curved claws make digging through tough soil easy.

They dig to find food underground. They can dig through hard, sun-baked ground in just a few minutes. This helps them uncover rodents, insects, and reptiles hiding in burrows. No burrow is safe from a hungry honey badger!

Honey badgers also dig to reach underground beehives. They tear open nests to eat the bee larvae and honey inside.

BIG BULLIES

Hiss! A cobra rises up. A honey badger runs right at it!

Honey badgers are so fierce most larger predators leave them alone.

Big hunters stay away. Lions do not want to fight them. Leopards avoid them too. Honey badgers always fight back!

Hyenas will try to steal their food. But honey badgers fight hard. They bite. They scratch. They never give up.

One honey badger once fought off six lions and escaped! The lions could not hold onto its loose, thick skin.

FIGHT BACK

Screech! A honey badger faces a jackal. It stands its ground!

Honey badgers are fierce fighters. They try to escape danger first, but they will fight if cornered. When trapped, they turn and attack!

They use sharp teeth and claws as weapons. Their loose skin allows them to turn and bite an attacker who is biting them!

Honey badgers growl, hiss, and scream when threatened. This scares many predators away.

FUN FACT!

Honey badgers release a stinky smell from glands near their tail to repel enemies!

GO
ANYWHERE

Scrape! A honey badger climbs up a tree trunk. It moves fast!

Honey badgers can go almost anywhere. They walk, run, climb, and swim. Their strong legs help them travel far each night.

They climb trees to raid bird nests. Their sharp claws grip rough bark easily.

Honey badgers also swim across rivers. They paddle with all four legs. Water does not stop them!

Honey badgers can travel up to 20 miles in one night while searching for food. They rarely rest!

NIGHT SHIFT

Rustle! The sun is setting. A honey badger wakes up to hunt.

Honey badgers are **nocturnal**. They sleep during the hot day. When darkness comes, they wake up and start moving.

They hunt mostly at night. The cool air helps them stay active for hours. They search for food until morning.

Some honey badgers also move at dawn and dusk. This is called being **crepuscular**. These badgers rest in the middle of the night.

In the Kalahari Desert, honey badgers flip their schedule with the seasons! In hot summers, they hunt at night. In cold winters, they switch to hunting during the day.

LONE RANGERS

Honey badgers are such loners that they sleep in a different burrow almost every night! They wander their huge home ranges and never settle down in one spot.

Stomp! A honey badger walks alone. It needs no friends.

Honey badgers live by themselves. Each badger hunts alone. Each badger sleeps alone.

Males and females only meet to mate. Then they go their own ways.

Honey badgers have home ranges. These ranges overlap. Males roam about 210 square miles. Females use smaller spaces.

When two honey badgers meet, they are not always friendly. Males sometimes grunt and sniff each other, but meetings can turn into fights with lots of biting and scratching.

FINDING A MATE

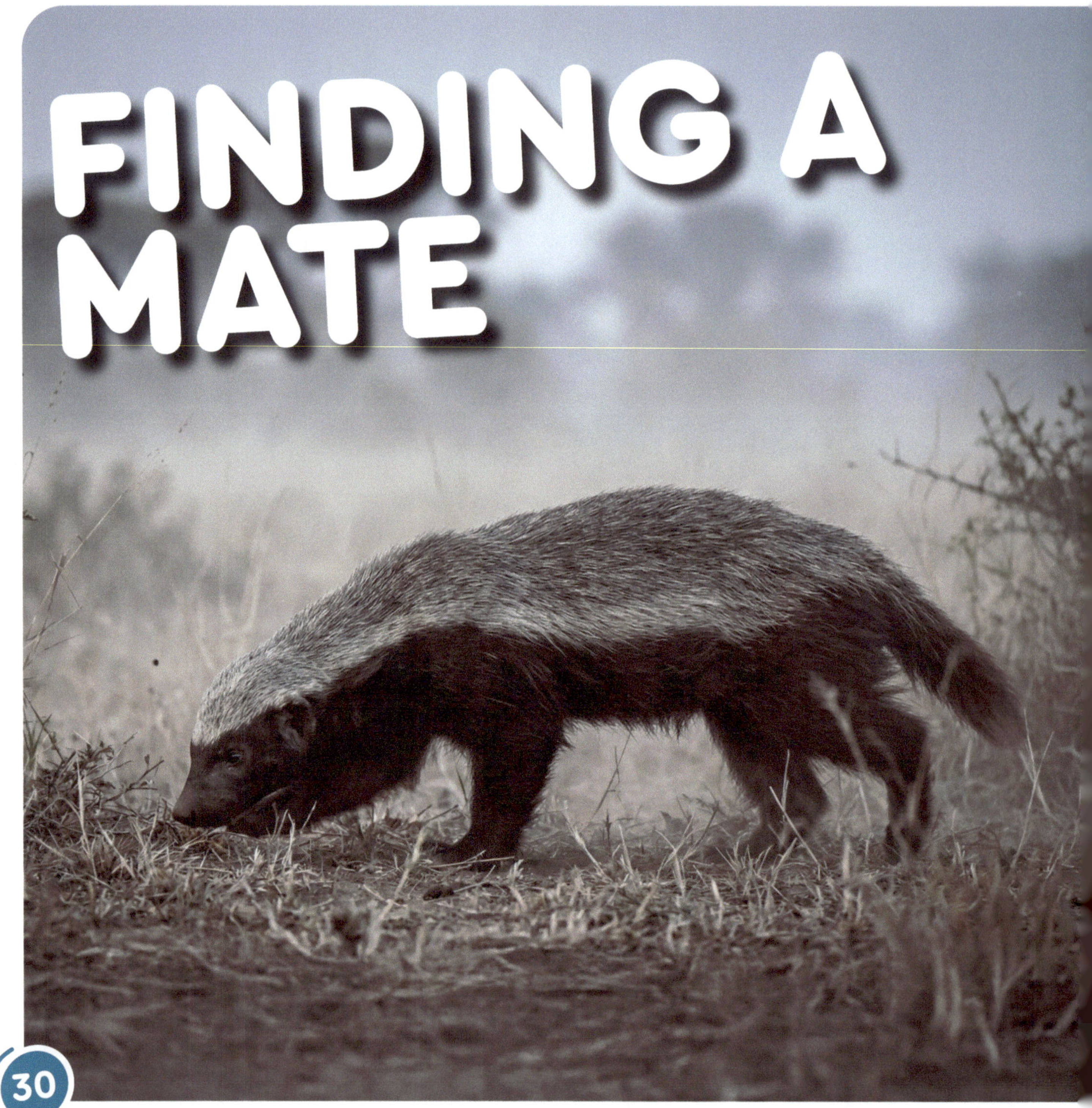

Grunt! A male honey badger sniffs the ground. He smells a female nearby.

Honey badgers can mate any time of year. Males travel far to find females. They follow scent trails left behind.

Males and females spend a short time together. They only stay together for a few days.

After mating, the male leaves. The female raises babies on her own. Honey badgers do not have the same partner every year.

Male honey badgers have powerful noses. They can smell a female from over a mile away.

TINY TERRORS

Squeak! A tiny honey badger kit peeks out of a burrow.

Baby honey badgers are called **kits**. A mother has only one or two at a time. They are born blind and helpless.

Kits stay in the den for about three months. Their eyes open after a few weeks, and the mother brings food to them.

Young honey badgers stay with their mother for over a year. She teaches them how to hunt and dig. Then they are ready to leave and live alone.

Honey badger cubs are born with no fur and weigh less than a tennis ball! They cannot see or hear at first.

BADGER BOOTCAMP

Snort! A mother honey badger carries her kit to a new burrow.

Mother honey badgers teach their young to survive. She shows her kit how to find food. She shows it how to dig burrows.

Kits watch their mother hunt. They learn to catch insects. They learn to catch lizards. They catch small mammals too. She also teaches them to break into beehives.

The mother shows her kit how to fight back. This helps young honey badgers grow brave and bold.

After about 14 months, the kit can live alone. It leaves to find its own territory.

FEARLESS FOREVER

Roar! A honey badger sees a big lion. It does not run away.

Honey badgers are very brave. They even hold the world record for the "world's bravest animal"!

These tough animals will attack lions and leopards. They fight hyenas too. They never give up. They keep fighting even when hurt and injured.

This helps them stay safe. Other animals leave honey badgers alone. Fighting one is too hard.

Honey badgers have attacked cars! They even chase people who get too close. They will fight any animal, big or small.

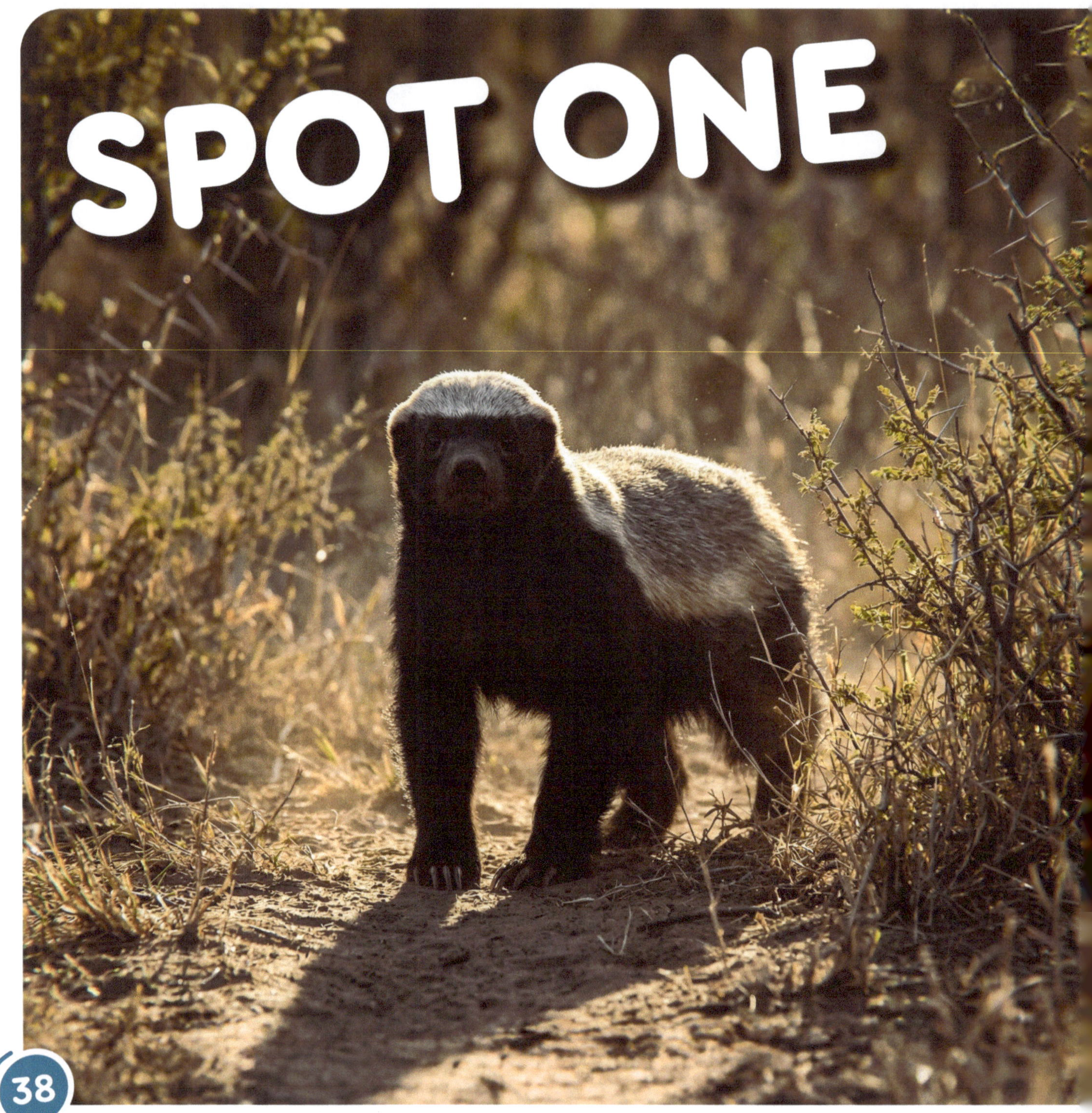

SPOT ONE

Click! A camera snaps. A honey badger is in the bush.

Honey badgers are hard to spot in the wild. They come out at night. They live far away in Africa and Asia.

But many zoos have honey badgers! Look for them in the small mammal house. Visit late in the day when they start to wake up.

Watch for a honey badger sniffing the ground. You might see one digging with its big claws. Ask the zookeeper for fun facts. They love to talk about these tough little animals!

FUN FACT!

One camera in Africa took a photo of the same honey badger 47 times in one month!

GLOSSARY

burrows
Holes or tunnels that animals dig in the ground to live in.

venomous
Having poison that can hurt other animals through a bite or sting.

nocturnal
Awake and active at night instead of during the day.

crepuscular
Active during dawn and dusk when the sun is rising or setting.

kits
Baby honey badgers.

www.ingramcontent.com/pod-product-compliance
Lightning Source LLC
Chambersburg PA
CBHW041614110726
48005CB00002B/396